CAMBRIDGE PRIMARY
Science

Learner's Book

4

Fiona Baxter, Liz Dilley,

CAMBRIDGE
UNIVERSITY PRESS

CAMBRIDGE
UNIVERSITY PRESS

University Printing House, Cambridge CB2 8BS, United Kingdom

One Liberty Plaza, 20th Floor, New York, NY 10006, USA

477 Williamstown Road, Port Melbourne, VIC 3207, Australia

314–321, 3rd Floor, Plot 3, Splendor Forum, Jasola District Centre, New Delhi – 110025, India

79 Anson Road, #06–04/06, Singapore 079906

Cambridge University Press is part of the University of Cambridge.

It furthers the University's mission by disseminating knowledge in the pursuit of education, learning and research at the highest international levels of excellence.

www.cambridge.org
Information on this title: www.cambridge.org/9781107674509

First published 2014

40 39 38 37 36 35 34 33 32 31 30 29 28 27 26 25 24 23 22

Printed in Malaysia by Vivar Printing

A catalogue record for this publication is available from the British Library

ISBN 978-1-107-67450-9 Paperback

....

Introduction

The *Cambridge Primary Science* series has been developed to match the Cambridge International Examinations Primary Science curriculum framework. It is a fun, flexible and easy to use course that gives both learners and teachers the support they need. In keeping with the aims of the curriculum itself, it encourages learners to be actively engaged with the content, and develop enquiry skills as well as subject knowledge.

This Learner's Book for Stage 4 covers all the content from Stage 4 of the curriculum framework. The topics are covered in the order in which they are presented in the curriculum for easy navigation, but can be taught in any order that is appropriate to you.

Throughout the book you will find ideas for practical activities, which will help learners to develop their Scientific Enquiry skills as well as introduce them to the thrill of scientific discovery.

The 'Talk about it!' question in each topic can be used as a starting point for classroom discussion, encouraging learners to use the scientific vocabulary and develop their understanding.

'Check your progress' questions at the end of each unit can be used to assess learners' understanding. Learners who will be taking the Cambridge Primary Progression test for Stage 4 will find these questions useful preparation.

We strongly advise you to use the Teacher's Resource for Stage 4, ISBN 978-1-107-66151-6, alongside this book. This resource contains extensive guidance on all the topics, ideas for classroom activities, and guidance notes on all the activities presented in this Learner's Book. You will also find a large collection of worksheets, and answers to all the questions from the Stage 4 products.

Also available is the Activity Book for Stage 4, ISBN 978-1-107-65665-9. This book offers a variety of exercises to help learners consolidate understanding, practise vocabulary, apply knowledge to new situations and develop enquiry skills. Learners can complete the exercises in class or be given them as homework.

We hope you enjoy using this series.

With best wishes,
the Cambridge Primary Science team.

Contents

1 Humans and animals

1.1 Skeletons

Sometimes skeletons look scary. Skeletons are not scary. People, and many animals, have a skeleton inside their bodies. A skeleton is a hard, strong frame that supports our bodies from the inside.

Have you seen a skeleton before? There are skeletons in some museums of animals such as dinosaurs that lived long ago.

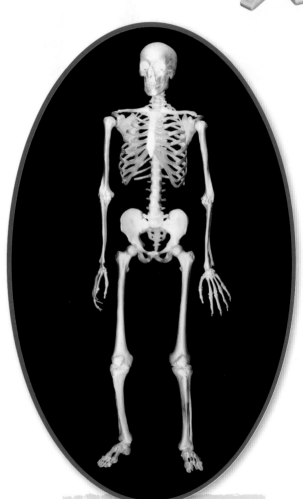

Our skeletons are made of many different bones. These bones are different sizes and shapes.

What are skeletons made of?

Skeletons are made of bone. Bone is very hard and strong.

You can feel the bones of your skeleton through your skin.

Finding your bones

Feel your head. How many skull bones can you feel?

Hold your hands on the sides of your chest. Can you find your ribs?
How many ribs can you feel?

Now feel your back. The bumps you can feel are the bones
of your spine. These bones are called vertebrae. One bone is called a vertebra.

Stand up and put your hands on your hips. Can you feel your hip bones?

Feel your hand bones. Why do you think there are so many bones in
your hand?

Did all the bones in your hand feel the same size and shape?

Questions

1   What are skeletons made of?

2   Why must skeletons be hard and strong?

3   Why do you think the bones of your
    skeleton are different shapes and sizes?

4   Bones are not very heavy. How do you
    think this helps animals?

5   Draw a picture of what you think a person
    without a skeleton might look like.

Animal skeletons have bones that
are different shapes and sizes.

Talk about it!

Are all skeletons
made of bones?

What you have learnt

- People and many other animals have a
  skeleton inside their bodies.

- Our skeletons support our bodies from the inside.

- Our skeletons are made of many different bones.

- Bones are different sizes and shapes.

1.2 The human skeleton

We have 206 bones in our skeletons. There are different kinds of bones in the skeleton:

Words to learn

thigh   irregular

- Long bones, like the bones in our legs and arms. The thigh bone is the long bone in your leg.
- Short bones, like those in our fingers.
- Flat bones, like those that make up our skull.
- Irregular bones, like the bones in our spine.

Activity 1.2

Making a skeleton

You will need:
different shapes of pasta • black construction paper • paper glue

Look at the human skeleton on the opposite page.
Notice the sizes and shapes of the bones
and how they are arranged.
Plan how you will make a skeleton from different pasta shapes.
Arrange the pasta shapes on the paper to make your skeleton.
When you are happy with your skeleton, glue the shapes onto the paper.

Questions

1 Is the skull made of one bone or many bones?
2 Why do you think the skull is important?
3 Which is the biggest bone in the body? Why do you think this is so?
4 Which are the smallest bones in the body?
5 What parts of your body do you think the ribs surround? Why do you think the ribs are there?
6 Women usually have wider hip bones than men. Why do you think this is so?

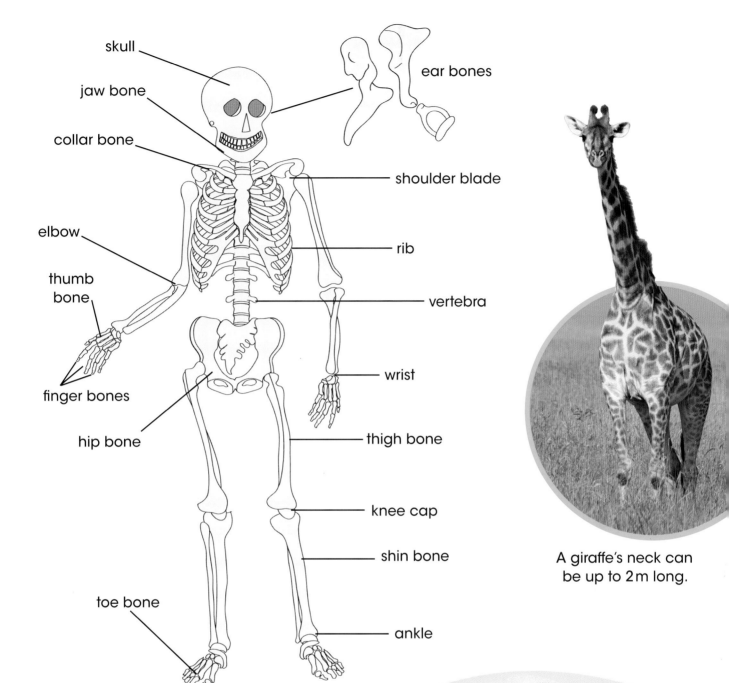

skull

jaw bone

collar bone

elbow

thumb bone

finger bones

hip bone

toe bone

ear bones

shoulder blade

rib

vertebra

wrist

thigh bone

knee cap

shin bone

ankle

A giraffe's neck can be up to 2m long.

Talk about it!

How many neck bones does a giraffe have?

What you have learnt

🌀 Our skeletons are made of long bones, short bones, flat bones and irregular bones.

🌀 The skull is made of different flat bones joined together.

1.3 Why do we need a skeleton?

Skeletons grow

Words to learn
fracture   X-ray
invertebrate

We grow and get bigger because our skeleton grows. An adult's skeleton is much bigger than a child's skeleton. An adult's skeleton has stopped growing.

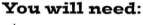

Activity 1.3

Comparing bone sizes

You will need:
a tape measure

Using a tape measure, measure the length of your:

● upper arm bone   ● thigh bone   ● shin bone.

Measure the length of the cut-outs of the same bones on your teacher.

Record your measurements in a table like this one.

Bone	Length in cm	
	Me	Teacher
upper arm bone		
thigh bone		
shin bone		

Whose bones are longer?

Predict what you think the length of a teenager's bones would be and say why.

Sometimes we fall or have accidents and break our bones. A broken bone is called a fracture. Doctors take a special photo called an X-ray to see if a bone is broken or not. X-rays are photos that let us see inside our bodies.

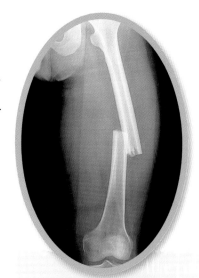

This X-ray photo shows a broken leg. Bones don't stay broken. The broken ends of the bone slowly grow back together again.

Skeletons support and protect

Our skeleton supports our body. It makes a strong frame inside the body. We cannot squash our body easily because of our skeleton. It gives our body shape and makes it firm. Our skeleton also protects our organs.

Do all animals have skeletons?

Not all animals have a skeleton. Worms and jellyfish do not have a skeleton. An animal with no skeleton is called an invertebrate.

Jellyfishes do not have a skeleton.

Questions

1 What would happen to a baby if its skeleton did not grow?
2 Why do broken bones mend?

What you have learnt

- We grow because our skeleton grows.
- The skeleton supports and protects the body.
- Animals without skeletons are called invertebrates.

Talk about it!
Why do fractures in old people take much longer to heal than fractures in children?

1.4 Skeletons and movement

Muscles make us move

Bones are strong and hard. They cannot bend but your body can move in many ways.

Our bodies can move in many ways.

All animals with skeletons have muscles attached to the bones. Muscles are the parts of the body that allow us to move in many different ways.

Muscles are found under the skin. They cover the skeleton and give your body the shape that you have.

Muscles always work in pairs. One muscle contracts and pulls on the bone it is joined to. This makes the bone move. The opposite muscle relaxes.

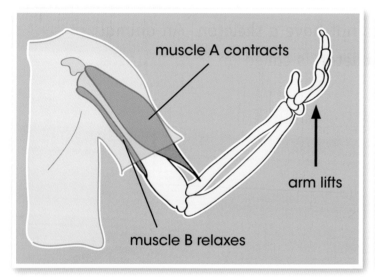

muscle A contracts

arm lifts

muscle B relaxes

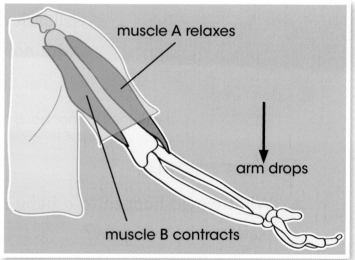

muscle A relaxes

arm drops

muscle B contracts

How muscles work

Muscles pull on bones to make them move. Muscles work by getting shorter and longer. When muscles get shorter, they pull on the bones they are joined to. We say that muscles contract. The pulling movement allows you to move and do the action that you want.

When muscles relax they get longer and let you rest.

Activity 1.4

How muscles work

You will need
a weight to lift, such as large book

Look closely at the muscles in your arm and at the pictures opposite.

Hold the weight in one hand and slowly lift the weight up towards you.

Put your other hand over the front on your upper arm.

Feel how the muscle changes as you lift the weight.

How does the muscle at the back of your arm feel?

Straighten your arm. Feel what happens to the muscle at the back of your arm. What happens to the muscle at the front of your arm?

Questions

1. How strong are your arm muscles? Design a fair test to find out.

2. Why is the heart not joined to any bones?

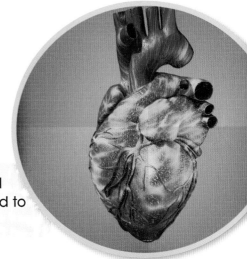

The heart is a special muscle that is not joined to any bones.

Talk about it!
How can we make muscles bigger?

What you have learnt

- Muscles allow us to move.
- Muscles are joined to bones.
- Muscles work by pulling on bones.
- Muscles work in pairs.

1.5 Drugs as medicines

Drugs

Drugs are substances that make your body change in some way. Many drugs have good effects but some drugs can harm your body.

Tobacco is the drug in cigarettes. Tobacco can harm the lungs.

Medicines

When people are unwell they take medicine.
We take medicines to help make us feel better when we have an illness. Some medicines also prevent us from getting ill.

Not all drugs are medicines. Tobacco, for example, is not a medicine.

How we take medicines

We take different kinds of medicines in different ways.

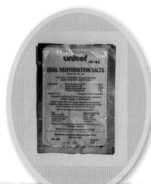

Some medicines come as a powder that we have to mix with water.

We breathe in medicines from inhalers for asthma and other breathing problems.

We drink cough medicine to help us to stop coughing.

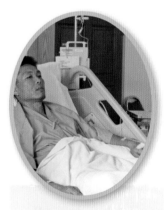

People who are very ill in hospital often get their medicine directly into their blood through a drip.

Activity 1.5

How do people take medicines?

Plan and carry out an investigation to find out the
different ways that people you know take medicines.
How will you collect the information you need?
How will you present your findings?

Questions

1   Why do we say that all medicines are drugs, but not all drugs are
    medicines?

2   Do you think we can use a cream as a medicine for a sore throat?
    Say why or why not.

3   Why do you think people in hospital often get their medicine
    through a drip?

Challenge

Smoking is harmful. Find out how
smoking damages the body.

Talk about it!

How does an inhaler
help you to
breathe better?

What you have learnt

- Drugs are substances that make your body
  change in some way.
- Medicines are drugs that make our bodies better
  when we are sick.
- All medicines are drugs, but not all drugs are medicines.
- We can take medicines in different ways, such as powders mixed
  with water, by inhalers and directly into our blood.

1.6 How medicines work

Symptoms and cures

How do you know when you have the flu? When we are ill, we have signs of the illness called symptoms. Different illnesses have different symptoms.

Look at the picture below to see some of the symptoms of flu. One of these symptoms is a fever. Medicines help to take away the symptoms of the illness.

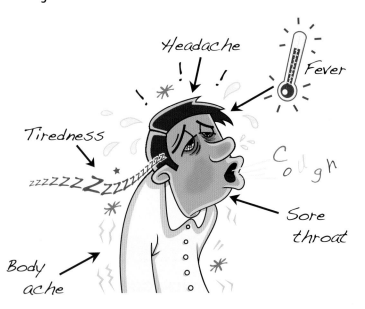

Often we become ill because germs enter our body. Medicines can help to kill the germs and make the illness go away. When medicines make an illness go away, we say that the medicines cure us.

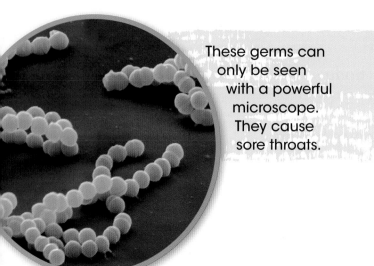

These germs can only be seen with a powerful microscope. They cause sore throats.

Medicines make us better but we have to take them safely. You should only take medicines if they are given to you by a doctor, a nurse or an adult who looks after you. Sometimes a doctor will prescribe medicines.

Taking medicines safely

Jimmy and his friends talked about how to take medicines safely.
These are their ideas.

It's okay to take someone else's medicine if they have the same illness as you.

You must always take the right amount of medicine. If you take too much it can be harmful.

If you forget to take your medicine in the morning just take more at lunchtime.

If the instructions tell you to take the medicine with food, you must make sure that you do.

Discuss what Jimmy and his friends are saying about how to take medicines safely and decide if they are right or not. You might need to find out more information about this. Make an information sheet about how to take medicines safely.

Question

1   Predict what you think would happen if you didn't take all the medicine the doctor prescribed for you.

Talk about it!

Why must some medicines be prescribed by a doctor?

What you have learnt

- Symptoms are the signs of illness.
- Medicines can cure illnesses and make them go away.
- We must follow the instructions to take medicines safely.

Check your progress

1 Write down the word that describes each of the following:

  a A frame made of bone that supports our body.
  b A bone in the spine.
  c The bones of the head.
  d Animals with no skeleton.
  e The parts of the body that allow our bones to move.

2 Write down the name of one:

  a flat bone
  b long bone
  c short bone
  d irregular bone.

3 Look at the drawing and answer the questions.

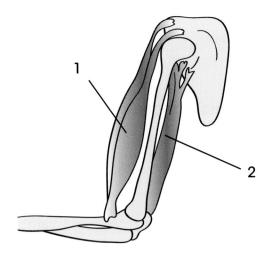

  a Write down the number of the muscle that bends the arm.
  b Explain how the muscle makes the arm bend.
  c What happens to the other muscle when the arm bends?

4 Josie, Yasmin and Luisa measured the length of their upper arm bones. These are their results.

	Josie	Yasmin	Luisa
Bone length in cm	25	32	28

    a Who do you think is an adult?

    b Who do you think is a teenager?

    c Who do you think is a child?

    d Explain your answers to questions a–c.

    e How else could you show these results?

    f What apparatus do you need to measure bone length?

    g Explain how you can make this a fair test.

5 a Name two reasons why we take medicines.

    b Which of these statements about medicines are true?

      A All medicines are drugs.

      B Medicines give us symptoms of illnesses.

      C Never take medicines prescribed for someone else.

      D Medicines can kill harmful germs in the body.

      E Stop taking prescribed medicines when you start to feel better.

2 Living things and environments

2.1 Amazing birds

These birds live in very different places.

Sharp eyes for hunting.

Powerful wings for lifting prey.

Sharp talons for holding and tearing at flesh.

Some eagles can kill and carry away small sheep.

Eyes are sharp underwater for hunting fish.

Sharp bill for catching fish.

Thick feathers to keep in body heat.

Webbed feet for swimming.

Emperor penguins live at the South Pole in temperatures as cold as –40 °C in winds of up to 100 km per hour.

Sharp eyes for hunting.

Smooth body shape for high speed.

Shaped beak for catching insects.

Wings tuck in for high speed.

The swift can fly at up to 170 km per hour.

Each bird's body is adapted to help them survive in their habitat.

The habitat is the local environment that they live in.

What do you think birds need from their habitat?

Activity 2.1

Bird watching

Make a plan for bird watching near your school.
Where will you do this? What will you need? Will you need to attract
birds? How will you do this?
How much time is needed?
Think about how you will
make sure you do not
frighten the birds.
Decide what records
you need to make.

Then spend some time observing birds and making records.
Try watching birds at different times of day.
Is there a time when you observe more birds?

Questions

1 How does the shape of a bird's beak help it to eat its food?

2 Why do birds need good eyesight?

3 Why do some birds have webbed feet?

Talk about it!

How are birds
adapted to
their habitat?

What you have learnt

◌ Birds are adapted to help them live in
their habitats.

2.2 A habitat for snails

Can you see the snail's shell? Can you see its eye stalks, mouth, and foot?

foot   head

Snails eat the leaves, stems, roots and fruits of plants.

They have no teeth. They have rough tongues which they use to eat leaves.

They have moist skin that must not dry out.

They live under stones, rocks and leaves.

If the environment gets very dry, snails move back into their shells.

Snails can change the way they behave if the environment changes.

How could we observe snails to see where they like to live?

Challenge

If snails disappeared from their habitat, what would happen to the birds that like eating snails?

Questions

1   How do snails protect themselves when the environment is too dry?

2   How is a bird that eats snails suited to the place in which it lives?

Activity 2.2

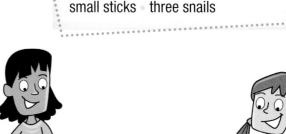
You will need:
a tray · leaves · dry stones · sand
small sticks · three snails

What habitat do snails like?

Design a choice tray like the one in the picture. Plan how you will test some snails to see where they like to be. How will you make the test fair? Think about each variable such as the colour of the tray, the light, the moisture and the surface of the tray. Do snails like dry places or damp

places? Make a prediction.
Look for any pattern or trend in the results. Repeat the tests to get more useful results. Present your results as a bar chart.

Snail shells are often black or brown. How might this colouring be useful to the snail?

Some birds are adapted to eat snails. They have good eyesight; they can move quickly and have strong beaks.

What you have learnt

- Animals, such as snails, are suited in different ways to the place they live.
- If the environment changes, animals can sometimes change the way they behave.

Talk about it!
How do snails protect themselves from being eaten?

2.3 Animals in local habitats

Some animals eat plants. Some animals eat other animals. Animals must live in a habitat where they can find food.
Here is a woodland habitat.

Word to learn
woodland

Rabbits, ducks and swans eat plants.
Foxes, hawks and owls eat other animals.

Can you think of **three** other animals that only eat plants?
Can you think of **three** other animals that eat other animals?

Activity 2.3

Observing local animals

You will need:
paper · pencils

Walk around the school garden, local park, woodland or meadow. How could you investigate which animals live there? What science questions would you ask about the animals? Draw and write notes about the animals.

Talk about the animals and how they are suited to the local environment.
Can you describe their habitat?
Do some animals prefer one habitat?
Do you see a pattern in your results?

Questions

1. Name **three** local habitats. You might choose a wet grassy area, or the bark of a tree.

2. How are animals adapted to live in these habitats?

What you have learnt

- Animals need a habitat where there is food.
- Some animals eat plants. Some animals eat other animals.

Talk about it!

Why do more birds visit a garden that has lots of insects?

2.4 Identification keys

There are millions of animals in the world and scientists have to be able to identify them. They need to sort animals into groups.

Scientists also have to be able to identify animals. They do this with an identification key. There are keys for animals and keys for plants.

Here is an identification key. Each box has a question. By answering the questions, we can identify a bird, a cat, a fish and a snake.

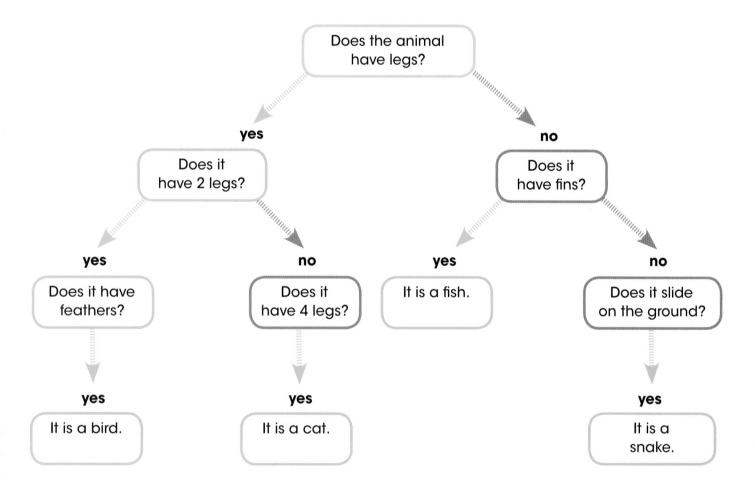

Making a key

Draw a key which will
help you to identify a tiger,
shark duck and goat.

Questions

1   How does an identification key help us?

2   What **two** answers can be given to a question in an identification key?

3   How could you extend the key opposite to include a rabbit?

4   Find out the names of some groups of animals. For example, what is the
name of the group that includes both humans and cats?

Challenge

Choose four animals. Draw a key to help
you identify your animals.

Talk about it!
How would you make
a key big enough for
all the animals in
your country?

What you have learnt

- Scientists need to be able to group animals.
- We can use an identification key to group animals.

2.5 Identifying invertebrates

Most invertebrates are small and hard to see. They hide among grass, plants, leaves, sticks and in soil.

An insect is an invertebrate. Insects have six legs and can often fly. Ants, butterflies, greenflies and bees are insects.

Before scientists can make a key, they have to observe the animals very carefully.

An earthworm is an invertebrate but it is not an insect.

Bees are insects that produce honey.

This butterfly has six legs and two wings.

Ants work together in colonies.

Questions

1 What is an insect?

2 Is there more than one way to group animals? Explain your answer.

3 Do animals know which group they are in? Explain your answer.

Activity 2.5a

Observing invertebrates

Collect invertebrates from different places around your school.

Why should you spend the same time collecting from each place?

Decide how you will record your observations.

Invertebrates are very small, so be careful. Use a pooter to help you. It will not harm them.

Carefully observe the invertebrates' shape, colour, number of legs, head, mouth, each antenna, shell, skin, and how they move.

Discuss any questions you have about them and how you could find the answers.

Activity 2.5b

Design an invertebrate hotel

Design an invertebrate hotel that you could build in the school grounds. Say why you think the invertebrates will like this hotel.

Talk about it!

What questions would you include on a key to identify invertebrates?

What you have learnt

- Invertebrates hide among grass, leaves, plants, sticks and in soil.
- We can use identification keys to group invertebrates.

The Earth is home to more than seven billion people.

It is also home to billions of animals and plants.

People, plants and animals need clean air and water.
All of us need to use energy. We also make a lot of waste.

People affect the Earth in both good and bad ways. The picture shows some of the bad ways.

Words to learn

energy   waste
natural disaster
man-made disaster
protect

An earthquake can kill animals and plants. It is an example of a natural disaster.

If an oil tanker sinks, the oil spills into the ocean. This can kill thousands of sea creatures and sea birds. This is called a man-made disaster.

We can all help to protect the environment.

Activity 2.6

How can we help the environment?

Look around your school and the local environment.
Look for things that could damage the environment.
Look at lights, waste bins, heating, water waste, air conditioning and toilet waste pipes.
In your local environment, can you see local factories, farms, homes, roads, railways or ships?
Make drawings of these and then label your drawings. Think about how these things have can have a bad effect on the environment.
How could you reduce the bad effects?

Railways can be good for the environment because they can reduce the number of vehicles on the roads.

Questions

1 Make a list of human activities that affect the environment.

2 Write down some ways in which you can protect your own environment.

3 What is a natural disaster? Give an example.

Talk about it!

How can we protect the environment?

What you have learnt

- People affect the environment.
- People, other animals and plants all need clean air and water.
- Natural disasters affect the environment but are not caused by people.

2.7 Wonderful water

Most of the water on Earth is salty.
This means that we can't drink it.

Some people do not have enough clean fresh water to drink.

We need clean fresh water to drink. We need it for our animals to drink and for our plants.

We do not always look after our fresh water.
Villages, towns and cities pollute rivers.

People and animals make waste which pollutes the river water. The animals and plants in the river die and the water is not safe to drink. People who drink polluted water, or eat the fish from polluted water, can become sick or can die.

Rivers often begin in the mountains where the water is clean and safe. Lots of animals and plants live in and by the rivers.

By stopping pollution we can make the land and waters clean again.

Activity 2.7a

Your own river

You will need:
a large piece of paper • pens • pencils

Make a large poster of the life of a river as it flows from the mountains, through forests, lakes and past towns, farms and factories.
Give your river a name.
Discuss the animals and plants that might live in the river and how they might suffer from pollution.
Write on your poster to explain what is happening to the river.

Cleaning the water

Look at the pictures to see what to do.
You may want to repeat this activity.
Why might this be a good idea? Does the water look cleaner?

Observe some fresh, clean tap water.

Stir in some clean sand to pollute the water. Observe how the water has changed. Can you see that is it cloudy?

Use a funnel and filter paper to pass the water through the filter paper. Collect the water.

Questions

1 What causes river pollution?
2 What can happen to the animals and plants in a polluted river?
3 What can happen to people who drink polluted water?

What you have learnt

- Clean, fresh water is important to humans, other animals and plants.
- People often pollute fresh water.
- Polluted water can harm people, animals and plants.

Talk about it!
What do people drink where there is no clean water?

2.8 Recycling can save the Earth!

Humans make a lot of waste. We throw away clothes that could be reused. A lot of waste is buried. This pollutes the soil and the ground water. Some materials can be recycled so that they don't have to be buried.

Glass recycling
The waste glass is used to make new glass bottles.

Paper recycling
The waste paper goes to make new paper.

Plastic recycling
The waste plastic goes to make new plastic things.

General waste
This type of waste is buried and will pollute the soil and ground water.

Gardeners and farmers recycle plant material by making compost heaps. They pile up dead plant material.

Micro-organisms use the dead plant material as food. This is what we call rotting.

As the plant material rots, it turns into compost. Compost helps plants to grow when it is added to soil.

Activity 2.8a

You will need:
plastic gloves · leaves · plant stems
an apple core · a plastic bag or jar with a lid

Making a mini compost heap

Gather some plant materials. Put them in a plastic bag or jar. Add a little water. Close the bag or jar. Micro-organisms will begin to eat the plant material. Observe the changes over a number of days. Record your observations.

Activity 2.8b

You will need:
paper · a pen · access to the internet or books about sea life and pollution

Plastic waste kills sea life

Research the effects of plastic waste on sea creatures. Use books and the internet. Write a report on what you find out. Explain how the plastic gets into the sea and how the plastic harms sea creatures.

Suggest what could be done to help the situation.

Questions

1. Why should we make compost heaps?
2. Why is it important to recycle materials?

Talk about it!
How could you encourage people to recycle more glass and plastic bottles?

What you have learnt

- When waste is buried it pollutes the soil and groundwater.
- Some materials can be reused and some can be recycled.
- Plant materials can be recycled into compost.

2 Check your progress

1   a   Write the name of the habitat shown in each picture.

    b   Say why the animal shown is suited to live in each habitat.

2   Look at this animal and the features of its body. Write down how you think its body is suited to its habitat.

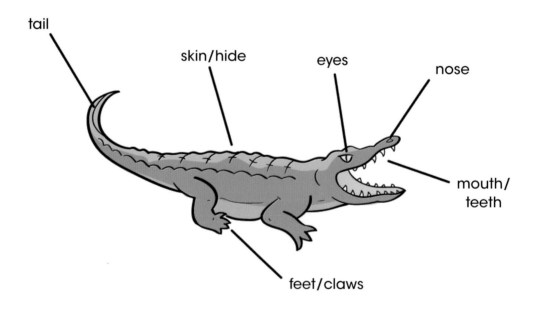

3 Construct a key to identify these pets.

4 Each day, Tabansi the farmer dumps manure from his animals on the land next to the river. The bar chart shows how many tonnes he dumps each day in one week.

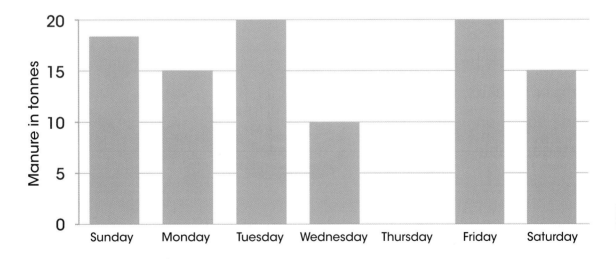

a On which day was there least pollution?

b On which days was there most pollution?

c How would this pollution affect the river?

3 Solids, liquids and gases

3.1 Matter

What is matter?

Matter is everything around us.

A brick is a solid.

Water is a liquid.

The air inside the bubble is a gas.

Matter exists in three different states. A state of matter is called a phase. These phases are known as solid, liquid or gas.

It is Suni's tenth birthday party. Identify two solids, two gases and one liquid on his birthday table.

Gases in air

Air is everywhere around us. Air is a mixture of different gases. We can't see or smell the gases in air. A gas called nitrogen makes up $\frac{4}{5}$ of the air.

Air also contains a gas called oxygen. We need oxygen to live. We breathe in oxygen. We breathe out a gas called carbon dioxide, which is also found in air.

Some gases do have a colour. Some gases also have a smell.
Hydrogen sulfide smells like rotten eggs.

Hydrogen
sulfide

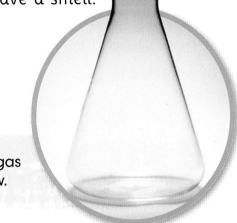

Chlorine gas
is yellow.

Activity 3.1

Making carbon dioxide

You will need:
vinegar · bicarbonate of soda
· a glass bottle · a surgical or
rubber glove · an elastic band

Put some bicarbonate of soda in a surgical or
rubber glove. Then, fill the glass bottle halfway
with vinegar. Attach the glove carefully to the bottle using an elastic band.
Ensure that you do not mix the bicarbonate of soda and the vinegar whilst
attaching the glove. Once attached, shake the bicarbonate of soda into the
vinegar. Observe what happens. The gas you have made is carbon dioxide.

Questions

1   What state of matter is:

   a vinegar   b bicarbonate of soda   c produced in the reaction?

2   Draw a picture to show what happened when the vinegar
    and bicarbonate of soda mixed together.
    Label the liquid and the gas.

Talk about it!

How do you decide if
something is a solid, a
liquid or a gas?

What you have learnt

- Matter is everything around us.
- Matter can exist in three different phases:
  solid, liquid or gas.
- Air is a mixture of different gases.

3.2 Matter is made of particles

A particle is a very small part of something.

Scientists can use a scientific model to explain how and why something happens. The particle model is a good way to explain the differences between solids, liquids and gases.

This model says that all matter is made up of particles. In real life, the particles in matter are too small to see. In the model we can show the particles as little balls.

The particles in matter are always moving, even in things that look still. The amount of movement of the particles decides whether something is a solid, liquid or gas.

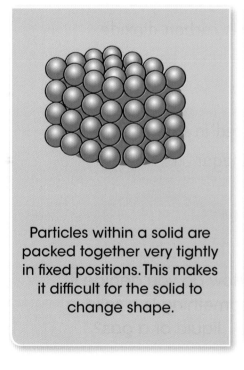

Particles within a solid are packed together very tightly in fixed positions. This makes it difficult for the solid to change shape.

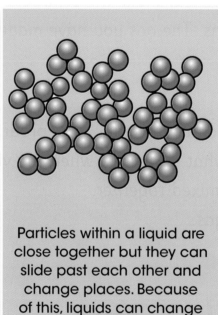

Particles within a liquid are close together but they can slide past each other and change places. Because of this, liquids can change shape easily.

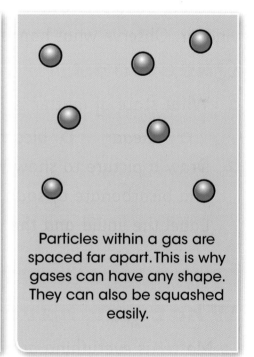

Particles within a gas are spaced far apart. This is why gases can have any shape. They can also be squashed easily.

The particle game

Divide into groups. Imagine that each person in your group is a particle in a solid, a liquid or a gas. Look at the pictures to see what to do.

solid

liquid

gas

Try to shake from side to side. What do you notice?

Try to move closer together or further apart. What do you notice?

Try to change the shape of your group. What do you notice?

Now change group and repeat the activity.

Questions

1 Compare what happened when you tried to shake as solids, liquids and gases.

2 What happened when you tried to move closer together in each case?

3 What happened when you tried to change the shape of each of your groups?

Talk about it!

How does the particle game demonstrate the particle model of matter?

What you have learnt

- All matter is made up of particles.
- Solids keep their shape as the particles do not change position.
- Liquids can change their shape as the particles are able to slide past each other.
- Gases can have any shape as the particles move far away from each other.
- Gases take on the shape of their container.

Can matter change its shape?

Word to learn

pour   bubble

Solids

Try to squeeze your desk, chair or pencil. Can you make it a different shape?

Most solids can't be squashed into a different shape. Remember the particle model. Particles within a solid are packed closely together. There is no space for the particles to take on a different shape.

Liquids

Predict what will happen when you pour some water onto a flat surface.

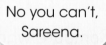

Ameena, I can make water change its shape.

No you can't, Sareena.

Activity 3.3a

Prove that water can change its shape

Plan a demonstration to prove that water can change its shape when you pour it.

Decide on the equipment you will use and what you will do.

Now carry out the demonstration.

Use the particle model to explain why liquids can change their shape.

Gases

If gases are contained in something they take on the shape of the container. Look at the picture. Here the gas is contained inside the bubble. When there is no container gases spread out.

Activity 3.3b

Observing how gases behave

Dip the ring into the soapy water. Blow air through the ring to make bubbles.

What is the gas inside the bubbles?

What happens to the gas when the bubble bursts?

Questions

1 a Draw a picture of particles of air inside a bubble.

   b Draw the same number of particles of air when the bubble bursts.

2 Why can't you change the shape of a brick by squeezing it?

3 Draw a labelled diagram to explain how a puddle forms when it rains.

Challenge

Gas is sometimes used as a fuel for cooking. Why do we keep this gas in sealed metal containers?

Talk about it!

How do you think it is possible to squeeze some solids into different shapes?

What you have learnt

- Most solids do not change shape.
- Liquids take the shape of the container they are in or spread out over a surface.
- Gases only have a shape when they are contained within something.

Words to learn

melting   freezing
steam   boil

Sabera's ice-cream started as a frozen solid. When the sun heated the ice-cream it changed to a liquid. This change from solid to liquid is called melting.

Water exists in three different phases: ice (solid), water (liquid) and water vapour (gas), which we often call steam.

We can show melting in this way:

solid ————— heat causes melting —————→ liquid

Freezing is the opposite of melting. Freezing is when something changes from a liquid to a solid.

Activity 3.4a

You will need:
ice cubes • pot (pan or saucepan)
hot plate

What happens to ice when it is heated?

Put the ice cubes into the pot.
Heat the pot on the hot plate.
Predict what you think will happen to the ice.
What does happen to the ice?
This is the phase change the ice goes through when you heat it:

Safety Be careful of the hot plate, it can burn you. Steam can also burn you.

solid phase (ice) ——— heat ———→ liquid phase (water)

Now heat the water until it starts to boil.
Observe how the water changes.

Activity 3.4b

What happens to steam when it is cooled?

Your teacher will hold the shiny board in the steam.

Predict what you think
will happen to the steam.
Observe what happens.

Safety

Be careful of the steam,
it can burn you.

Put the liquid you collect in the freezer for 30 min.
Predict what will happen to it.

Questions

1 Copy and complete the sentence below. Fill in the phase changes the water went through when it cooled down.

steam (_____ phase) ⎯⎯⎯ cool down ⎯⎯→ _____ (_____ phase)

2 What happens to the water when you put it in the freezer?

3 Copy and complete the sentence below. Fill in the phase changes the water went through when it froze.

water (_____ phase) ⎯⎯⎯ cool down ⎯⎯→ _____ (_____ phase)

Talk about it!
How does the particle model help us to understand melting and freezing?

What you have learnt

- Melting occurs when a solid is heated and it changes into a liquid.
- Boiling occurs when a liquid is heated and it changes into a gas.
- Freezing occurs when a liquid is cooled and it changes into a solid.

3.5 Melting in different solids

Activity 3.5

Word to learn
gold

You will need:
an ice cube · a square of chocolate
a cube of butter · three pans · three
hot plates · a stop-watch or digital
watch

Be careful of the hot
plate, it can burn you.

Safety

Compare melting in different solids

Place an ice cube in a pan. Do the same with
the chocolate and the butter.

Predict which substance you think will melt
first when you heat it.

Start heating each substance at the same
time. Record the time you start.

Observe carefully. Record the time taken for
each substance to completely melt.

melting ice

melting chocolate

melting butter

Record your results in a bar chart.

Questions

1 Describe the phase change that each substance went through
   when you heated it.

2 How did you try to make this investigation a fair test?

3 In what ways was the investigation not a fair test?

4 What will happen to the water if you continue heating it?

Even metals like gold and iron will melt if they get hot enough. Metals have to be heated in a furnace to melt. When the melted metal cools it becomes a solid again.

This gold was heated until it melted. Then it was poured into moulds.

The gold cools in the mould and becomes a solid again. These solid gold bars are called ingots.

Here are the phase changes the gold has passed through:

solid ——— heat ———→ liquid ——— cool ———→ solid

Talk about it!

Why do you think different substances take different times to melt?

What you have learnt

- Some solids take longer to melt than others.
- Even metals melt if they get hot enough.

3.6 Melting and boiling points

Every substance melts and boils. Different substances take different times to melt because it takes different amounts of heat to melt them. The amount of heat in a substance is called the temperature.

The temperature at which a substance melts is its melting point. This is when it changes from a solid to a liquid.

The temperature at which a substance boils is its boiling point. This is when it changes from a liquid to a gas.

Words to learn

melting point   boiling point

This is water boiling. Water has a boiling point of 100 °C.

We measure temperature with a thermometer. The unit we use is degrees centigrade, °C.

Activity 3.6

Measuring the temperature of water

Put some water in a cup. Measure the temperature of the water with the thermometer. Record the temperature in °C. This is the temperature of the water at room temperature.

You will need:
water • a cup • ice cubes
a pan • a hot plate • a
thermometer • tongs

Put the ice cubes in a pan and heat them. As soon as the ice cubes have melted, remove the pan from the hot plate. Take the temperature of the water. Record the temperature. This is the melting point. Now heat the water until it boils. Take the temperature of the steam. Record the temperature. This is the boiling point.

Safety Be careful of the steam, it can burn you.

Questions

1 What temperatures did you record for:
   a the melting point of water
   b the boiling point of water
   c water at room temperature?

2 Draw a bar chart to show these three temperatures.

3 The melting point of water is 0°C and the boiling point is 100°C. Did you measure these temperatures? If not, why do you think the temperatures you measured were different?

4 Why should you never put your hand in steam?

What you have learnt

- The boiling point is the temperature at which a substance changes from a liquid to a gas.
- The melting point is the temperature at which a substance changes from a solid to a liquid.

Talk about it!
How does the particle model help to explain a melting point?

3 Check your progress

1 Which of the following substances are solids? Which are liquids and which are gases?

oil   plastic   paper   carbon dioxide   oxygen   vinegar

2 Which of these statements describes a solid, a liquid or a gas?

a Takes on the shape of the container.
b Spreads out in all directions.
c Does not change shape easily.
d Is often colourless.
e Cannot be squashed.

3 a What are the three phases of water?
   b What is the boiling point of water?
   c What is the melting point of ice?

4 a Does the diagram below represent a model of a solid, a liquid or a gas?
   b Write a sentence to explain your answer.

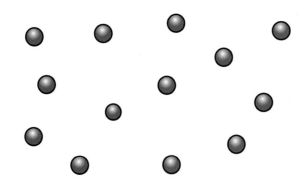

5 Amul and Jiao want to compare how long it takes to melt margarine and butter. They want to plan a fair test.

a Which of these actions should they take? You can choose more than one.

A Put equal amounts of butter and margarine together in a pan.

B Put equal amounts of butter and margarine in a pan and a pot.

C Put equal amounts of butter and margarine in two identical pans.

D Heat both pans one after the other on the same stove.

E Heat each pan on an identical stove starting at the same time.

F Heat one pan on a gas ring and the other pan on an electric plate starting at the same time.

b Draw diagrams to describe how the butter changes from a solid to a liquid. Use the particle model in your diagrams.

4 Sound

Sounds come from sources

Words to learn

source   travel

Sunita hears an aeroplane passing overhead.

The aeroplane is a source of sound.
Sunita hears the sound when it enters her ears.

The sound can travel from the aeroplane to Sunita's ears.

Activity 4.1

Make a tin can telephone

You will need:
a piece of string about 3 m long • two empty tin cans

Look at the pictures to see what to do.

1

Use the string to join the two tin cans.

2

Give one tin can to a partner. Keep the other one yourself. Walk away from your partner until the string is tight.

3

Talk softly into your tin can. Your partner should listen into their tin can. Did your partner hear your voice? This is how the tin can telephone works.

Sound travels through different materials

Sound travels through materials, like string.
Sound can travel through different kinds of materials.

Questions

1 What is the source of sound in the tin can telephone?

2 Which materials does the sound travel through in the tin can telephone?

3 Why did the Native American people lie with one ear in the ground to listen for enemies or animals to hunt?

Talk about it!

Why do you think outer space is completely silent?

What you have learnt

- Sounds come from sources.
- Sound travels from a source to our ears.
- Sounds travels through materials like string.

4.2 Sound travels through different materials

Activity 4.2

You will need:
a source of sound, like a ticking clock • a balloon filled with water • a block of wood or a wooden door

Investigating how sound travels through different materials

Sound travels better through some materials than through others.

Look at the pictures to see what to do. Remember to stand the same distance away from the clock each time.

Listen carefully. How well did you hear the sound each time? Draw a table like the one shown. In the table record how well you heard the sound through the different materials.

1 air

Cover one ear. Can you hear the clock ticking?

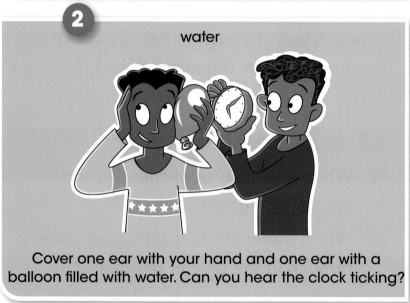

2 water

Cover one ear with your hand and one ear with a balloon filled with water. Can you hear the clock ticking?

3 wood

Cover one ear with your hand and put the other ear against a block of wood. Can you hear the clock ticking?

Show how loud the sound was by using ticks:

✓ = soft   ✓ ✓ = louder   ✓ ✓ ✓ = loudest

Material	Loudness of sound
air	
water	
wood	

Questions

1   Which material did you hear the sound best through?

2   How did you make the investigation a fair test?

Whales communicate with each other under water. The sounds travel a very long way.

Challenge

Describe how you could investigate whether sound travels best through wood, plastic or metal.

Talk about it!

Why do you think sound travels best through solids?

What you have learnt

- Sound travels through different materials.
- Sound travels through solids, liquids and gases.
- Sound travels best though solids.

4.3 How sound travels

Sound travels through different materials. But how does sound travel?

Words to learn
vibrate   vibration

Activity 4.3

Jumping rice

You will need:
plastic wrap · elastic bands · rice grains · an empty glass jar · a metal baking tray · a wooden spoon · a pencil

Put the plastic wrap over the top of the jar. Keep the wrap in place with an elastic band. Sprinkle a few rice grains over the wrap.

Hit the side of the jar with the pencil. What happens to the rice?
Hold the tin tray close to the jar and bang it with a spoon. What happens to the rice?

Predict what will happen if you clap your hands next to the jar. Try it out. Was your prediction correct?

Vibrations cause sounds

Sounds are made when things vibrate. A vibration is a very quick movement back and forth. You often cannot see vibrations, but you can feel them. Hold your hand in the middle of your throat and hum a tune. You will feel the vibrations and hear the sound.

You can see these guitar strings vibrate.

Sound travels because vibrations travel

Why did the rice grains in Activity 4.3 move?

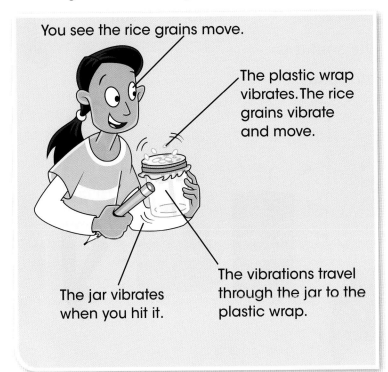

You see the rice grains move.

The plastic wrap vibrates. The rice grains vibrate and move.

The jar vibrates when you hit it.

The vibrations travel through the jar to the plastic wrap.

The tin tray vibrates when you hit it.

The air around the tin tray vibrates.

Questions

1 Did you hear a sound when you hit the jar? Why?

2 Think back to the tin can telephone. Which materials vibrated when you used the telephone?

Talk about it!

How could you stop the sound travelling in a tin can telephone?

What you have learnt

- Vibrating objects make sounds.
- Vibrations move from the vibrating object through materials.
- We hear sounds when the vibrations reach our ears.
- Sound travels because vibrations travel.

4.4 Loud and soft sounds

How can we make sound louder?

Words to learn
loud   soft

Look at the picture. Do you think the sound is loud or soft? What makes the sound louder?

A motorbike starting up is a loud sound.

A whisper is a soft sound.

Activity 4.4a

Listening to sound through a tube

You will need:
a long cardboard tube · a source of sound

Look at the pictures. Copy what the children in the pictures are doing.

Hold the clock next to my ear so that I can listen to the tick.

1

Can you hear the clock now?

2

Can you hear the clock now? Is it louder or softer than before?

3

Questions

1 Was the sound of the clock louder or softer when you moved the clock further from your ear? Why do you think that this happened? Use the words vibrations, travel and air in your answer.

2 Was the sound louder through the tube? Why do you think that this happened?

Activity 4.4b

Planning a fair test for loud and soft sounds

Think of a question about loud and soft sounds.
Plan a fair test to find the answer to your question using everyday materials.
In your plan, list the materials you would use and the steps you would take.
Explain how you would make it a fair test.
Suggest how you would present your results.

This is the oldest type of music player with no electronic parts.

Question

1 Look at the picture. How do you think the music was made louder?

What you have learnt

◎ Sounds can be loud or soft.
◎ Trapping the sound vibrations makes the sound louder.

Talk about it!

How do people in your community deal with loud sounds?

4.5 Sound volume

A sound is louder when the vibrations are bigger. The volume of a sound is how loud or soft it is.

Words to learn

volume   decibel
sound level meter

A decibel (dB) is the unit we use to measure the volume of sound.

These are the volumes of some everyday sounds. Very loud sounds (louder than 85 dB) can damage our ears.

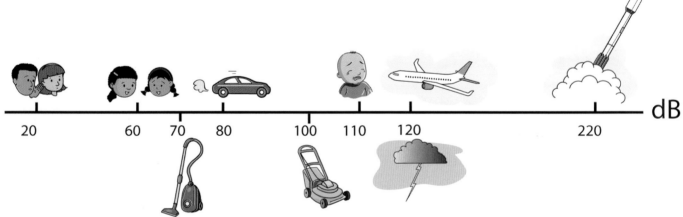

Measuring sound volume

Some people play loud music. How can you find out how loud the music is? You can use a sound level meter.

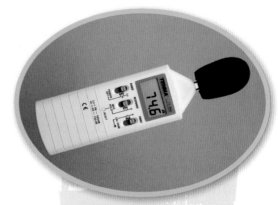

A sound level meter.

Activity 4.5

Measuring sounds

You will need:
a sound level meter • ways to make different sounds

Think of some sounds to measure, for example, clapping hands, blowing a whistle, slamming a door or the class talking. Predict which sound will be loudest and which will be softest.
Plan how you will measure the sounds.
How will you make sure that the test is fair?
Plan how you will record the sounds.
Will you use a table or a bar chart?

Challenges

1 Predict the volume of silence in decibels.

2 How can you find out if your prediction is true?

Questions

1 Which sound was loudest?

2 Which sound was softest?

3 Were your predictions correct?

4 Explain why some sounds are loud and other sounds are soft.

Talk about it!
How does a sound level meter measure volume?

What you have learnt

- Small vibrations cause soft sounds.
- Large vibrations cause loud sounds.
- The volume of a sound is how loud or soft the sound is.
- We measure sound in units called decibels.
- We can use a sound level meter to measure the volume of sounds.

4.6 Muffling sounds

There are some sounds that we don't like or sounds that are too loud. We can muffle sounds that we don't want to hear. This means that we make the sounds quieter and less clear.

Words to learn

muffle   ear defenders
silencers

Loud sounds can hurt our ears. Some people work in very noisy places. They need to protect their ears. They wear ear defenders to muffle sound.

The sound of this jack hammer is very loud.

The volume of sound from an electric hand drill could damage ears.

The sound inside an aeroplane can be very loud.

Ways to muffle sound

We fit silencers to cars, trucks and motor cycles to muffle the sounds of their engines.

In buildings we use carpets and curtains to stop noise. Sometimes the spaces between walls are filled with materials that don't let noise through.

This motorbike silencer muffles the sounds of the engine.

4 Sound

Finding out which material muffles sound the best

Predict which material will muffle sound the best.

Place the sound source in the box. Pack one of the materials around the sound source in the box. Then place the lid on the box.

Stand about 1 m away from the box and listen to the sound. Is the sound loud or soft?

sound source

newspaper

shoe box

put the lid on the shoe box and stand 1 m away

If you have a sound level meter, measure the sound volume and record it.

Repeat the activity with the other materials. Present your results in a table.

Questions

1 Which material muffled sound the best? Why do you think so?

2 Was your prediction correct?

3 Is this investigation a fair test? Explain why or why not.

Talk about it!

Why can it be dangerous to listen to music through earphones while riding your bicycle?

What you have learnt

- Some materials can muffle sounds well.
- Some materials are not good at muffling sounds.

4.7 High and low sounds

Pitch

A whistle makes a high-pitched sound. Thunder makes a low-pitched sound.

Slow vibrations produce a low-pitched sound. Fast vibrations produce a high-pitched sound.

Pitch is not the same as volume. The volume describes how loud or soft the sound is. For example, the sound of thunder is low-pitched but also loud.

Some sounds have such a high pitch or such a low pitch that we cannot hear them.

Elephants make very low-pitched sounds that we cannot hear. But other elephants can hear these sounds up to 7.5 km away.

Bats make high-pitched sounds that we cannot hear.

String instruments

A guitar is a string instrument. Some strings are thicker than others. The guitar has pegs that you can use to make the string tighter or looser. You can also make the strings shorter by pressing them down. These things change the pitch of the notes. When you 'tune' a string instrument you change the pitch of the strings so that it is right for each string.

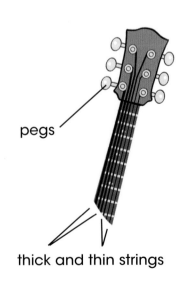

pegs

thick and thin strings

Making high-pitched and low-pitched sounds on a guitar

Pluck the thick strings and the thin strings.
Which strings make a higher pitched note?
Tighten one of the strings by turning the peg.
Now pluck the string. Does the sound have a higher or
a lower pitch than before?
Loosen the string by turning the peg the other way.

Predict the pitch of the sound when you pluck the string.
Now pluck the string. Was your prediction correct?
Now press the strings down on the neck with the fingers
of one hand while you pluck the strings with your other hand.
How does the pitch change?

Questions

1 Which factors affect the pitch of the sound of a stringed instrument?

2 Which has a higher pitch: a long string or a short string?

3 Which has a lower pitch:
   a thin string or a thick string?

Talk about it!
How could you 'tune'
a guitar to make the
pitch of the notes
sound right?

What you have learnt

🌀 The pitch of a sound is how high or how
   low that sound is.

🌀 The faster the vibrations, the higher the pitch of the sound.

🌀 You can raise the pitch on a stringed instrument by making
   the string thinner, shorter or tighter.

4.8 Pitch on percussion instruments

Percussion instruments include drums, shakers and rattles. Drums are one of the oldest and simplest musical instruments.

To make a sound with a percussion instrument, like a drum, you have to hit or shake it. Hitting or shaking it sets up vibrations in the air and you make a sound.

A daf is a drum from the Middle East.

Look at each of these instruments. Which of these have you seen and heard?

maracas   tambourine   bongos

Some drums have a 'skin' stretched over the top. When you stretch the skin tightly, it makes the vibrations quicker.

The drums in the steel band are made from metal oil drums.

The drums in the steel band are different sizes. When you hit the top of one of the drums the metal top vibrates and makes a sound. The air trapped in the drum makes the sound loud.

Questions

1 In the steel band, which drums do you think make high-pitched sounds and which make low-pitched sounds?

2 How does the steel band play a tune?

3 How could you change the pitch of the sound on the African drum in the picture?

What you have learnt

- Banging a small drum makes fast vibrations and a higher pitched note.
- Tightening the drum skin also gives a higher pitched note.

Talk about it!

What could you use to make your own percussion band?

4.9 Having fun with wind instruments

Each of these pictures shows a woodwind instrument. Some have one pipe and others have many pipes.

Words to learn
woodwind instrument

People make music from woodwind instruments by blowing down or across the tops of hollow pipes. This makes the air vibrate inside the pipe to make a sound.

A recorder from the UK. The recorder has one pipe. You have to change the length of air in the pipe to make high- and low-pitched notes. You can block the air holes in the pipe to do this.

A didjeridu from Australia.

A shakuhachi from Japan.

A dizi from China.

Sometimes woodwind instruments consist of a line of pipes of different lengths. These are pan pipes from Bolivia.

Activity 4.9

You will need:
eight glass bottles or jars of the same size
water and food colouring · a large jug

Making sounds by blowing

Line your bottles up on a table.

You are going to make your own wind instrument and use it to change the pitch of the sound.

Pour water into the jug and colour it with a few drops of food colouring.

Pour water into each bottle like in the picture.

Pour a little water into this bottle.

Pour a little more water into this bottle.

This bottle must be almost full.

Column of air.

1   2   3   4   5   6   7   8

Gently blow across the top of each of the bottles 1–3.

Did you make sounds? Are the sounds from blowing across each of the three bottles the same pitch?

Predict what pitch of sounds you will make when you blow across the other bottles.

Collect evidence to test your prediction.

Talk about it!

How would you play the instruments shown on these two pages?

What you have learnt

- The pipe of a wind instrument traps air.
- Blowing across the top of the pipe makes the air vibrate, which makes a sound.
- The longer the column of air is, the lower the pitch of the sound.

1 Match up the words in column A with their meanings in column B.

A	B
volume	to make sounds less loud and less clear
vibrate	where something comes from
source	a unit for measuring sound
muffle	how high or low a sound is
pitch	how loud or soft a sound is
decibel	to shake very quickly backwards and forwards

2 Write down whether each of these sentences is true or false.

a You measure the volume of sound with a loudspeaker.

b You play a guitar by plucking the strings.

c Sound only travels through air.

d Soft materials are better than hard materials for muffling sound.

e Sound travels best through solids.

3 Look at the pictures of these musical instruments.

A   B   C

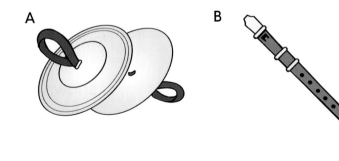

a Which instrument A, B or C can you play by:
  i   plucking
  ii hitting
  iii blowing?
b How can you change the pitch of the note with instrument B?

4 Describe each sound as high, low, soft or loud.

  a A whisper.
  b A bird singing.
  c A cow mooing.
  d An ambulance siren.

5 Faizah and Halima will use this apparatus to investigate how sound travels through solids, liquids and gases.

a Which container is full of gas? Which contains a solid and which contains a liquid?
b Why does each container have to be the same size?
c What will they use the clock for?
d How will they collect their evidence?
e What conclusion will they reach?

5 Electricity and magnetism

5.1 Electricity flows in circuits

Activity 5.1

You will need:
a torch with cells

Words to learn
cell   electricity
flow   current
complete circuit
terminal

Investigate a torch

If you turn on the torch what do you think will happen? Test your prediction.

What is inside the torch?
What do you think makes the light shine?

Safety

Be careful of cells. Do not open up any cell because the chemicals inside will burn you.

What is electricity?

The torch works because each cell pushes the electricity. This makes the bulb light up. Look at the picture of the inside of the torch.

Electricity can flow in one direction. We call this electrical current. You can think of current as particles travelling along a path. In the torch, the current flows from one end of the first cell to the other end. Then it flows through the next cell, through the bulb and back again into the first cell. Current needs a continuous path. This path is called a complete circuit.

What are cells?

A cell has a positive (+) and a negative (–) terminal. The current flows from the positive terminal to the negative terminal. If you use two cells, you must always put the negative terminal of one cell against the positive terminal of the other cell. Try this out with your torch.

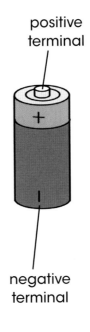

positive terminal

negative terminal

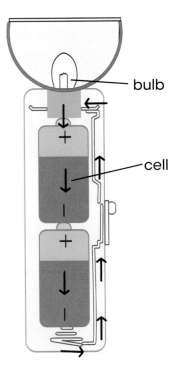

bulb

cell

The inside of a torch. The arrows show which way the electric current goes.

A car battery is a collection of cells.

Questions

1   What happens if you put the two positive terminals of the cells in a torch together? Will the bulb light up?

2   Explain why the cells in a torch have to be arranged with the negative terminal of one cell against the positive terminal of the other cell.

Talk about it!

What things do you use that need cells?

What you have learnt

- A cell pushes electric current around a circuit.
- Electric current flows from the positive to the negative end of a cell.
- You can think of current as particles flowing round the circuit.

5.2 Components and a simple circuit

Components

The bulb and the cell in a torch are each a component of a circuit.

You may have used these electrical components in Stage 2.

Each cell has a positive terminal (+) and a negative terminal (–).

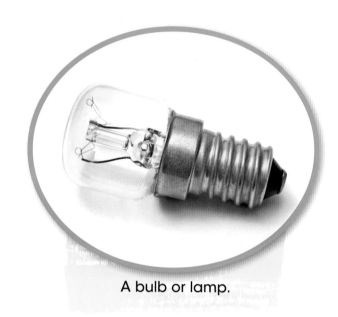

A bulb or lamp.

A bulb holder.

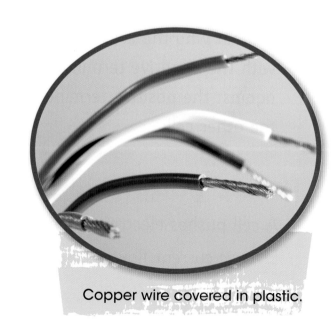

Copper wire covered in plastic.

Activity 5.2

Making a simple circuit

You will need:
a cell • a bulb in a bulb holder • wire
scissors or wire cutters • a knife or
wire strippers • tape 3 mm screwdriver

Cut the wire to make two lengths of 15 cm.

Strip the plastic coating from the ends of the wires with the knife or wire strippers until 2 cm is bare at all ends.

Be careful with the knife.
Always strip away
from you.

Safety

Look at the diagram. Predict what will happen to the bulb in this circuit.

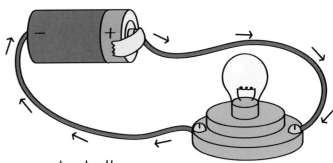

Make a circuit with one cell and one bulb as shown in the diagram. Observe the bulb. Predict what will happen to the bulb if you break the circuit by removing the tape and wire from one end of the cell.
Now break the circuit. Observe the bulb.

Questions

1 What happened to the bulb in your completed circuit? Explain why this happened.

2 What happened to the bulb when you broke the circuit? Explain why this happened.

Talk about it!

What would happen if you added another bulb to your circuit?

What you have learnt

⚬ A simple circuit is made up of components such as wire, a bulb and a cell.

5.3 Switches

Words to learn
switch

Sarena turns on the light switch. The switch closes the circuit and the light shines. When she turns off the switch, the circuit breaks and the light goes off.

A switch is another component in an electrical circuit. The switch turns the electric current on or off. It is the same idea as turning a tap on or off.

The circuit you made in Activity 5.2 had no switch. To break the circuit you took the taped wire off one of the cell terminals. A switch lets you turn a bulb on and off when you like, without having to break wires.

Activity 5.3a

Making a switch

Put together the parts as shown. Strip the plastic off the ends of the two pieces of wire. Wind one end of each piece of wire round the drawing pins as shown.

You will need:
a small block of wood • two metal drawing pins • wire • a sharp knife a metal paper clip

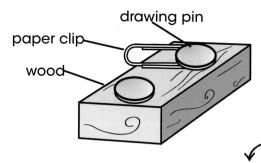

Press the paper clip down until it touches the other drawing pin. This completes the circuit. To switch off, lift the paper clip off the drawing pin. This breaks the circuit.

Making a circuit with a switch

Make a circuit like the one shown.
Predict what will happen when you close
the switch.

Close the switch. Observe the bulb. What happens?
If the bulb does not light up, check all your
connections in the circuit. Try again.

You will need:
a switch • a cell • a bulb
in a bulb holder • 30 cm wire
a sharp knife • scissors

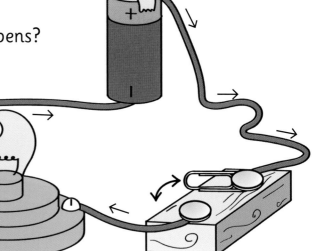

Questions

1 Why does the bulb light up when you close the switch?

2 What must you do with the switch to break the circuit?

3 Draw the circuit you made. Label the cell, the wire, the switch, the bulb and the bulb holder.

4 Why did you need to check your connections if the bulb did not light up?

Talk about it!
Where are switches used on electrical devices that you have seen?

What you have learnt

- Closing a switch completes a circuit and allows electric current to flow.
- Opening the switch breaks the circuit. This means the current will not flow.

Activity 5.4

Making a circuit with more components

So far you have made a circuit with one bulb and one cell.

Use tape to join two cells together to make a stronger cell. Make sure the positive and negative terminals are next to each other.

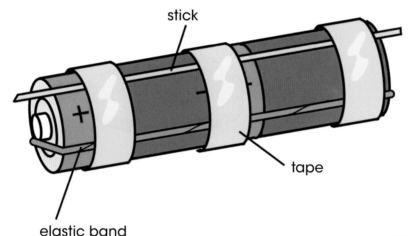

stick

tape

elastic band

Use the scissors to cut the wire into short lengths. Complete your circuit using three bulbs in bulb holders as shown.

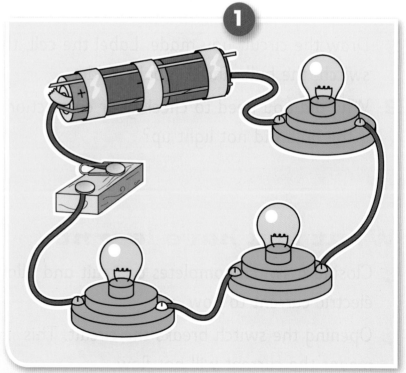

Close the switch. Observe the bulbs. Open the switch.

Remove one bulb and a bulb holder so that only two bulbs are left in your circuit.

Predict what would happen if you remove one more bulb in a bulb holder. This means that only one bulb remains in your circuit. Test your prediction. What happens to your bulb?

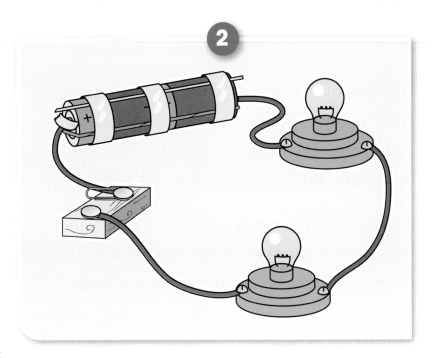

Questions

1 Did the bulbs shine more brightly or less brightly when you removed one bulb from the circuit? Why do you think this happened?

2 What happened when you only used one bulb in the circuit? Why do you think this happened?

3 Describe the path of the electricity in the circuit you made.

Talk about it!
Why may bulbs not light up in a circuit?

What you have learnt

☺ The bulbs shine less brightly when you add more bulbs to the circuit.

☺ If you have too many cells in the circuit, the bulbs pop or burn out.

5.5 Circuits with buzzers

In Activity 5.4, you left just one bulb in your circuit. The bulb probably popped or burnt out. This was because the source of electricity was too strong for one bulb.

Different components need different strengths of electricity. A buzzer is another component of a circuit. It needs a stronger supply of electricity than a bulb.

The strength of electricity is measured in a unit called a volt (V). The strength of electricity that a component needs for it to work is called the voltage.

This buzzer needs a supply of 3 V to work.

These cells have a strength of 1.5 V.

This bulb needs a supply of 1.5 V to work.

Activity 5.5

Making a circuit with a buzzer

If you put a 3 V buzzer into a circuit, you need a 3 V cell to make the buzzer work. You can make a 3 V supply by joining two 1.5 V cells.

You will need:

three 1.5 V cells • a 3 V buzzer a switch • wire • a knife scissors • tape • elastic band a stick

Check on the side of the buzzer to see which side is positive (+) and which side is negative (–). Connect the buzzer in the circuit so that the (+) terminal is connected to the (–) terminal of the cell.
Set up your circuit like the one shown in the picture.

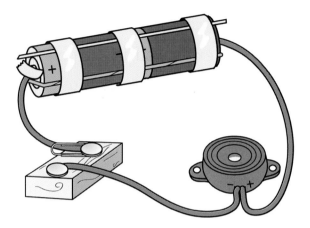

Test your circuit. Does the buzzer make a noise when you close the switch?
Take away one of the cells.
Test your circuit again.
Add two cells. Now your circuit has three cells. Test your circuit again.

Questions

1 How well did the buzzer work when you had three cells in the circuit?
2 How well did the buzzer work when you had one cell in the circuit?
3 Why do you need at least 3 V to make the buzzer work in your circuit?
4 You want to run an electric toy that has a voltage of 6 V. Why won't it work properly when you use a 1.5 V cell?

Talk about it!

What things do you use that need more than one cell?

What you have learnt

☺ Components such as bulbs and buzzers need a certain strength of electricity to be able to work.
☺ The voltage is the strength of the electricity.
☺ The cell must have a strong enough voltage for the components in the circuit to work.

5.6 Mains electricity

So far you have been using cells and components with voltages between 1.5 V and 3 V. These are safe to use. At home we have mains electricity.

This uses a much higher voltage (over 100 V). The exact voltage depends on your country. We use mains electricity for lights. We also use mains electricity to power an electrical appliance. Appliances must be plugged into a wall socket. Always turn a switch off before you take out a plug.

If mains electricity flows through your body you will get an electric shock. Mains electricity can also cause a fire if the plastic wears off the copper wires.

Electricity is only dangerous if you don't use it properly.

The lights in Hong Kong use a lot of electricity.

We can use mains electricity to charge new electric cars.

Safety rules

Never push anything, especially your fingers or a metal object, into a wall socket. You could get an electric shock.

Dry your hair outside the bathroom. Never use electrical appliances when your hands are wet or when you are in the bath. You could easily get an electric shock.

Look at the picture of the Mbatha family's kitchen.

Do not plug too many appliances into one socket. They will overload the socket and cause a fire.

Questions

1 Why should Thabo's mother dry her hands before she plugs in the toaster?

2 What is Thabo doing wrong at the wall socket?

3 Why is the wall socket behind the iron dangerous?

Talk about it!

What dangerous uses of electricity have you seen?

What you have learnt

- Mains electricity has a much stronger voltage than the electricity from cells.
- Never handle electrical appliances when you are wet.
- Follow the safety rules when using electricity.

5.7 Magnets in everyday life

Pedro is helping his grandmother pick up pins. He is doing it the easy way – he is using a bar magnet.

A magnet attracts some materials to it. We call these materials magnetic.

Types of magnet

Magnets come in many different shapes and sizes.

A horseshoe magnet is shaped like a horseshoe.

A wand magnet is shaped like a wand.

Some magnets are disc-shaped.

Some magnets are shaped like rings.

Finding out which materials are magnetic

Choose at least six things to test, for example, buttons and paper clips.
Plan a test to see which things are made from a magnetic material.
Carry out your test. Record your results in a table.
Are all materials magnetic? Use the evidence you have collected to answer this question.

Looking after magnets

Magnets lose their strength if you damage them. Make sure you don't drop them or bang them together. Store them in a box and cover the ends with a keeper.

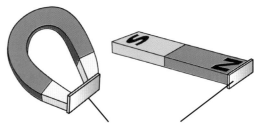

Use a keeper to keep magnets strong.

Lots of things we use every day have magnets inside them. The magnets attract metal parts and keep them in place. There are magnetics inside a television.

Questions

1 Name **three** different types of magnet.
2 Why should you not drop a magnet?

Talk about it!

What things do you have at home that contain magnets?

What you have learnt

- A magnet attracts some metal objects to it. These objects are magnetic.
- Objects not attracted to a magnet are non-magnetic.

5.8 Magnetic poles

Magnets have magnetic poles, called the north pole and the south pole. For example, on your bar magnets, the red end is the north pole and the blue end is the south pole. Attraction and repulsion are magnetic forces.

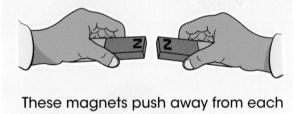

These magnets push away from each other. We call this repulsion.

Unlike poles pull towards each other. We call this attraction.

Activity 5.8a

Investigating bar magnets

You will need:
two bar magnets · string
scissors

Your magnets have ends marked in different colours, such as red and blue. Tie a piece of string round the middle of each bar magnet. Hold the end of a string in each hand so that the magnets swing.

When the magnets stop swinging, bring one magnet close to the other. Make sure that the end of one magnet faces the differently coloured end of the other magnet. What happens to the magnets?

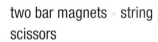

Hold the magnets so that two ends of the same colour face each other. What happens to the magnets?

Predict what will happen if you hold the magnets with the other two ends of the same colour facing each other. Test your prediction. Repeat this a few times to check your prediction.

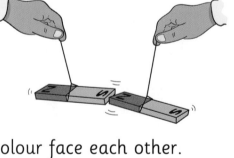

Activity 5.8b

You will need:

a horseshoe magnet
a bar magnet

Identifying the poles on a horseshoe magnet

The poles on your horseshoe magnet are not marked.
You can use a bar magnet to identify which end is the
north pole and which is the south pole.
Plan how you will do this.
Now carry out your test.

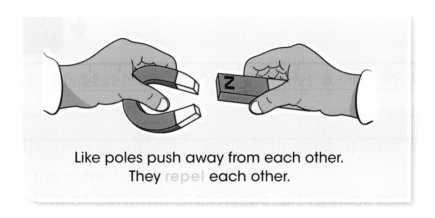

Like poles push away from each other.
They repel each other.

Questions

1 How did you carry out the test?

2 How did you decide which is the north pole and which is the south pole?

3 Draw the horseshoe magnet and label
   the poles north and south.

Talk about it!

Are a magnetic's north
and south poles the
same as the Earth's
North and
South Poles?

What you have learnt

- Magnets have a north pole and a south pole.
- Unlike poles attract and like poles repel each other.
- Attraction and repulsion are magnetic forces.

5.10 Which metals are magnetic?

Some metals are precious, such as silver, gold and platinum. These metals are expensive. Metals that we use in everyday life are iron, steel, aluminium, copper and chromium. Often things are made from a mixture of metals. A mixture of metals is called an alloy.

Words to learn

silver   steel
alloy

steel pipes

cast iron cook pots

Iron is used to make machines and cast iron cooking pots.

Steel is an alloy made mainly from iron. It is much stronger than iron. We use steel to make machines, steel pipes and bridges.

Aluminium is light in weight and does not rust. We use aluminium to make pans for cooking, aluminium foil and to build aeroplanes. Cans for cold drinks are also made of aluminium.

aeroplane

copper wire

stainless steel cutlery

brass door handle

Chromium is mixed with steel to make an alloy called stainless steel. Stainless steel does not rust. It has many uses such as knives, sinks and medical instruments.

Copper is used to make electric cables and wires.

Brass is an alloy of copper and zinc. We use brass to make door handles.

Activity 5.10

Are all metals magnetic?

Predict which objects you think will be magnetic. Test your prediction. Hold the magnet next to each of the metal objects. Observe whether the metal is magnetic or not.
Record your results in a table.

Questions

1 Name **two** magnetic metals.

2 Name **two** non-magnetic metals.

3 Give **three** examples of things you use at home that are made of metals. Which metals are they made from? Are these things magnetic or not?

4 How does the magnet seperate iron and steel from other metals?

The magnets attract metal cans made from iron and steel and separate them from the rest of the rubbish. Then the cans are recycled.

Talk about it!

How can you use magnets to sort steel and aluminium cans?

What you have learnt

- We use metals in everyday life.
- Mixtures of metals are called alloys. An example is brass.
- Iron and steel are magnetic. Many other metals are non-magnetic.

5 Check your progress

1 Write **one** word that each of the following describes.
   a Something that pushes electricity round a circuit.
   b The strength of electricity.
   c The flow of electricity.

2 Which of these are magnetic and which are non-magnetic?

   wood   copper   steel   plastic   aluminium   iron

3 a Name **two** components of an electric circuit.
   b Name **two** types of magnet.
   c Name **two** industrial uses of magnets.

4 In the circuit below:

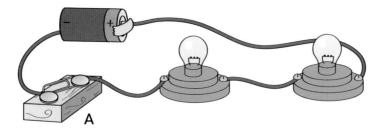

A

   a What is the function of the component marked A?
   b Is the current flowing clockwise or anticlockwise?
   c If you added a second bulb in a bulb holder would the bulbs glow more brightly or less brightly?
   d If you added two more 1.5V cells, what could happen to the bulbs?

5

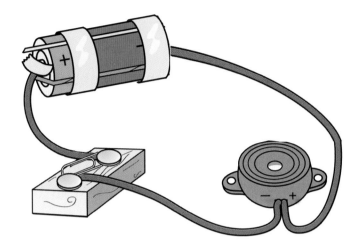

A 1.5 V cell is used with a 3 V buzzer. Will the buzzer work? Explain your answer.

6 Which of these statements are true and which are false?
   a You must never push anything into a wall socket.
   b It is safe to use an electrical appliance in a bathroom.
   c An electrical socket can have as many appliances as you like plugged into it.

7 Why does using a magnet help to pick up pins?

8 Describe how you could test the strength of magnets.

Reference

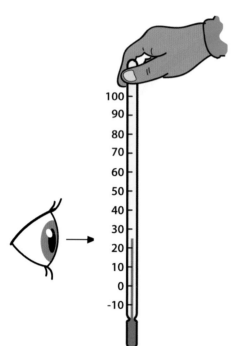

Hold the thermometer at the top.

Put your eye level with the top of the liquid in the thermometer to read the scale.

Do not hold the bulb as the thermometer will measure the temperature of your fingers.

How to use a thermometer to measure the temperature of a liquid

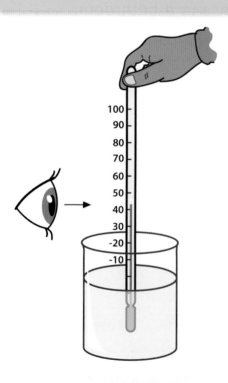

Hold the thermometer at the top.

Wait until the thermometer reading stops changing.

Read the scale before you take the thermometer out of the liquid.

Put your eye level with the top of the liquid in the thermometer to read the scale.

Make sure all of the bulb is in the liquid.

This liquid is at 43 °C.

Find the 'Start', 'Stop' and 'Reset' buttons on the stopwatch.

Check you can start, stop and reset the stopwatch.

Watch to see which digits count the seconds.

The two smaller digits count hundredths of a second.

Drisha and Idra are timing how long ice takes to melt.

The ice in the sun melted in just over three minutes and thirty five seconds.

The ice in the shade melted in five minutes forty eight and a half seconds.

How to plan a fair test

To plan a fair test you must only change one variable in the test. All other variables must be kept the same.

Suk and Pembe are investigating which materials are better at stopping sound.

The variable they are changing is the material being used.

To keep the test fair, Pembe must hold the materials the same way each time.

Suk must also keep the loudness of the triangle the same.

The distance from Pembe's ears to the triangle should also be the same.

How to design a bar chart

Olga and Sam have been counting the living things they find in the garden.

They have made a tally chart to show how many of each sort they have found.

	Number of living things found
birds	I I
worms	0
ants	⊦⊦⊦⊦ ⊦⊦⊦⊦ I I
spiders	⊦⊦⊦⊦

They want to draw a bar chart on squared paper.

First they have to draw the axes for the chart using a ruler.

To decide how tall to make the y-axis they look at how tall the bars will be. They saw 12 ants, so the tallest bar will go up to 12 on the y-axis.

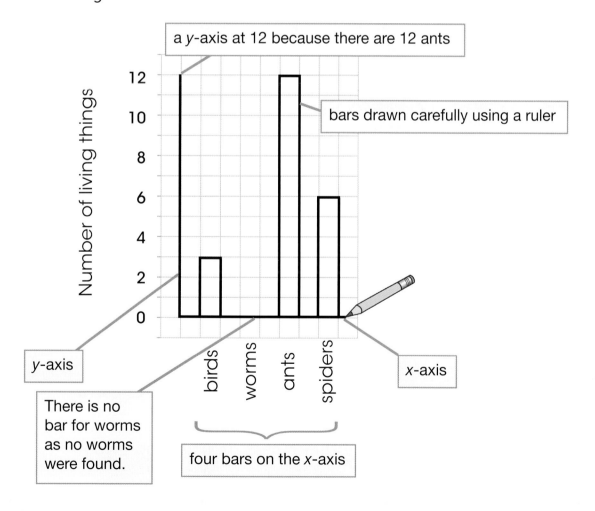

a y-axis at 12 because there are 12 ants

bars drawn carefully using a ruler

Number of living things

y-axis

x-axis

There is no bar for worms as no worms were found.

four bars on the x-axis

birds   worms   ants   spiders

Glossary and index

Acknowledgements

The authors and publisher are grateful for the permissions granted to reproduce copyright materials. While every effort has been made, it has not always been possible to identify the sources of all the materials used, or to trace all the copyright holders.
If any omissions are brought to our notice, we will be happy to include the appropriate acknowledgements on reprinting.
The publisher is grateful to the experienced teachers Mansoora Shoaib Shah, Lahore Grammar School, 55 Main, Gulberg, Lahore and Lynne Ransford for their careful reviewing of the content.

p. 6*l* Ingolf Pompe/LOOK Die Bildagentur der Fotografen GmbH/ Alamy; p. 6*r* David Arky/ Tetra Images/ Alamy; p. 7 Mark Evans/ iStockphoto; p. 9 andydidyk/ iStockphoto; p. 11*t* Praisaeng/ Shutterstock; p. 11*b* vilainecrevette/ iStockphoto; p. 12 Sean Murphy/The Image Bank/ Getty Images; p. 13 Ase/ Shutterstock; p. 14*tr* Grafissimo/ iStockphoto; p. 14*bl* Science Museum/ Science & Society Picture Library; p. 14*bcl* pelvidge/ iStockphoto; p. 14*bcr* Stockbroker/MBI/ Alamy; p. 14*br* kavida/ iStockphoto; p. 16 Eye of Science/ Science Photo Library; p. 28*tl* StudioSmart/ Shutterstock; p. 28*tc* Neale Cousland/ Shutterstock; p. 28*tr* vtupinamba/ iStockphoto; p. 28*br* Steve Shoup/ Shutterstock; p. 30*l* fotostory/ Shutterstock; p. 30*r* Richard Baker/In Pictures/Corbis News/ Corbis; p. 31 sgtphoto/ iStockphoto; p. 32*l* Hung Chung Chih/ Shutterstock; p. 32*r* Instryktor/ Shutterstock; p. 39 Charles D. Winters/ Science Photo Library; p. 44*tl* terekhov igor/ Shutterstock; p. 44*tr* Aleksandrs Samuilovs/ Shutterstock; p. 44*b* Tim UR/ Shutterstock; p. 47*l* CinemaHopeDesign/ iStockphoto; p. 47*r* elenstudio/ Shutterstock; p. 48*l* Charles D. Winters/ Science Photo Library; p. 48*r* scubaluna/ Shutterstock; p. 55 Denis Scott/Comet/ Corbis; p. 56 Andrew Lambert Photography/ Science Photo Library; p. 58*t* Ann and Steve Toon/ Alamy; p. 58*b* naluwan/ Shutterstock; p. 59 andrea crisante/ Shutterstock; p. 60 David J. Green - technology/ Alamy; p. 62*tl* tim gartside/ Alamy; p. 62*c* Blend Images/ SuperStock; p. 62*tr* Wave Royalty Free/Design Pics Inc/ Alamy; p. 62*br* Oleksiy Maksymenko/ Alamy; p. 64*l* Johan Swanepoel/ Shutterstock; p. 64*r* Ivan Kuzmin/ Alamy; p. 66*t* Kami Kami/ arabianEye/ Getty Images; p. 66*bl* Jose Luis Pelaez Inc/Blend Images/ Alamy; p. 66*bc* age fotostock/ SuperStock; p. 66*br* Jeff Greenberg333/ Alamy; p. 67 Robert Harding Picture Library/ SuperStock; p. 68*tl* Inspirestock Inc./ Alamy; p. 68*tr* Lynn Gail/Lonely Planet Images/ Getty Images; p. 68*c* LOOK Die Bildagentur der Fotografen GmbH/ Alamy; p. 68*bl* John Lander Photography/ Alamy; p. 68*br* Travel Pix/Taxi/ Getty Images; p. 73 Tjanze/ iStockphoto; p. 74*tl* Brooklin/ Shutterstock; p. 74*tr* inbj/ iStockphoto; p. 74*bl* Martyn F. Chillmaid/ Science Photo Library; p. 74*br* iStockphoto/ Thinkstock; p. 80*l* Djapeman/ iStockphoto; p. 80*tr* Kim Taylor and Jane Burton/Dorling Kindersley/ Getty Images; p. 80*br* Bob Mawby/ Shutterstock; p. 82*l* leungchopan/ Shutterstock; p. 82*r* Viappy/ Shutterstock; p. 83 Monkey Business Images/ Shutterstock; p. 84*l* Ivancovlad/ Shutterstock; p. 84*cl* Andre Adams/ Shutterstock; p. 84*cr* TEK Image/Science Photo Library/ Alamy; p. 84r Andrew Lambert/Leslie Garland Picture Library/ Alamy; p. 85 John Birdsall/ Alamy; p. 90*tl* DJ Srki/ Shutterstock; p. 90*tr* ivanastar/ iStockphoto; p. 90*cl* Fernando Jose V. Soares/ Shutterstock; p. 90*cr* Ted Foxx/ Alamy; p. 90*bl* venturecx/ iStockphoto; p. 90*br* Ross Fraser/ Alamy; p. 91 worradirek/ Shutterstock

Cover artwork: Bill Bolton

l = left, *r* = right, *t* = top, *b* = bottom, *c* = centre